Roller Coa: Log Book

MW01236175

This Book Belongs To:

Name: _____

Cell #: _____

Email: _____

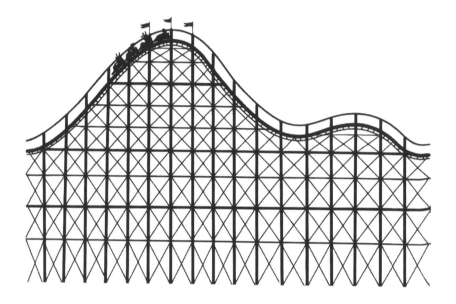

Roller Coaster Enthusiast Log Book

Amusement Park Name: _____

Location: _____

Date	Coaster Name	Height	Length	Speed	# Of Loops	Rate 1 to 5

My Ride Experience:

_____

_____

_____

_____

_____

Roller Coaster Enthusiast
Log Book

Amusement Park Name: _____

Location: _____

Date	Coaster Name	Height	Length	Speed	# Of Loops	Rate 1 to 5

My Ride Experience:

_____

_____

_____

_____

_____

Roller Coaster Enthusiast Log Book

Amusement Park Name: _____

Location: _____

Date	Coaster Name	Height	Length	Speed	# Of Loops	Rate 1 to 5

My Ride Experience:

_____

_____

_____

_____

_____

Roller Coaster Enthusiast Log Book

Amusement Park Name: _____

Location: _____

Date	Coaster Name	Height	Length	Speed	# Of Loops	Rate 1 to 5

My Ride Experience:

_____

_____

_____

_____

_____

Roller Coaster Enthusiast Log Book

Amusement Park Name: _____

Location: _____

Date	Coaster Name	Height	Length	Speed	# Of Loops	Rate 1 to 5

My Ride Experience:

_____

_____

_____

_____

_____

Roller Coaster Enthusiast Log Book

Amusement Park Name: _____

Location: _____

Date	Coaster Name	Height	Length	Speed	# Of Loops	Rate 1 to 5

My Ride Experience:

_____

_____

_____

_____

_____

Roller Coaster Enthusiast Log Book

Amusement Park Name: _____

Location: _____

Date	Coaster Name	Height	Length	Speed	# Of Loops	Rate 1 to 5

My Ride Experience:

_____

_____

_____

_____

_____

Roller Coaster Enthusiast Log Book

Amusement Park Name: _____

Location: _____

Date	Coaster Name	Height	Length	Speed	# Of Loops	Rate 1 to 5

My Ride Experience:

_____

_____

_____

_____

_____

Roller Coaster Enthusiast Log Book

Amusement Park Name: _____

Location: _____

Date	Coaster Name	Height	Length	Speed	# Of Loops	Rate 1 to 5

My Ride Experience:

_____

_____

_____

_____

_____

Roller Coaster Enthusiast Log Book

Amusement Park Name: _____

Location: _____

Date	Coaster Name	Height	Length	Speed	# Of Loops	Rate 1 to 5

My Ride Experience:

_____

_____

_____

_____

_____

Roller Coaster Enthusiast Log Book

Amusement Park Name: _____

Location: _____

Date	Coaster Name	Height	Length	Speed	# Of Loops	Rate 1 to 5

My Ride Experience:

_____

_____

_____

_____

_____

Roller Coaster Enthusiast Log Book

Amusement Park Name: _____

Location: _____

Date	Coaster Name	Height	Length	Speed	# Of Loops	Rate 1 to 5

My Ride Experience:

_____

_____

_____

_____

_____

Roller Coaster Enthusiast Log Book

Amusement Park Name: _____

Location: _____

Date	Coaster Name	Height	Length	Speed	# Of Loops	Rate 1 to 5

My Ride Experience:

_____

_____

_____

_____

_____

Roller Coaster Enthusiast Log Book

Amusement Park Name: _____

Location: _____

Date	Coaster Name	Height	Length	Speed	# Of Loops	Rate 1 to 5

My Ride Experience:

_____

_____

_____

_____

_____

Roller Coaster Enthusiast Log Book

Amusement Park Name: _____

Location: _____

Date	Coaster Name	Height	Length	Speed	# Of Loops	Rate 1 to 5

My Ride Experience:

_____

_____

_____

_____

_____

Roller Coaster Enthusiast Log Book

Amusement Park Name: _____

Location: _____

Date	Coaster Name	Height	Length	Speed	# Of Loops	Rate 1 to 5

My Ride Experience:

_____

_____

_____

_____

Roller Coaster Enthusiast Log Book

Amusement Park Name: _____

Location: _____

Date	Coaster Name	Height	Length	Speed	# Of Loops	Rate 1 to 5

My Ride Experience:

_____

_____

_____

_____

_____

Roller Coaster Enthusiast Log Book

Amusement Park Name: _____

Location: _____

Date	Coaster Name	Height	Length	Speed	# Of Loops	Rate 1 to 5

My Ride Experience:

_____

_____

_____

_____

_____

Roller Coaster Enthusiast
Log Book

Amusement Park Name: _____

Location: _____

Date	Coaster Name	Height	Length	Speed	# Of Loops	Rate 1 to 5

My Ride Experience:

_____

_____

_____

_____

_____

Roller Coaster Enthusiast Log Book

Amusement Park Name: _____

Location: _____

Date	Coaster Name	Height	Length	Speed	# Of Loops	Rate 1 to 5

My Ride Experience:

_____

_____

_____

_____

_____

Roller Coaster Enthusiast Log Book

Amusement Park Name: _____

Location: _____

Date	Coaster Name	Height	Length	Speed	# Of Loops	Rate 1 to 5

My Ride Experience:

_____

_____

_____

_____

_____

Roller Coaster Enthusiast Log Book

Amusement Park Name: _____

Location: _____

Date	Coaster Name	Height	Length	Speed	# Of Loops	Rate 1 to 5

My Ride Experience:

_____

_____

_____

_____

_____

Roller Coaster Enthusiast Log Book

Amusement Park Name: _____

Location: _____

Date	Coaster Name	Height	Length	Speed	# Of Loops	Rate 1 to 5

My Ride Experience:

_____

_____

_____

_____

_____

Roller Coaster Enthusiast Log Book

Amusement Park Name: _____

Location: _____

Date	Coaster Name	Height	Length	Speed	# Of Loops	Rate 1 to 5

My Ride Experience:

_____

_____

_____

_____

_____

Roller Coaster Enthusiast Log Book

Amusement Park Name: _____

Location: _____

Date	Coaster Name	Height	Length	Speed	# Of Loops	Rate 1 to 5

My Ride Experience:

_____

_____

_____

_____

_____

Roller Coaster Enthusiast Log Book

Amusement Park Name: _____

Location: _____

Date	Coaster Name	Height	Length	Speed	# Of Loops	Rate 1 to 5

My Ride Experience:

_____

_____

_____

_____

_____

Roller Coaster Enthusiast Log Book

Amusement Park Name: _____

Location: _____

Date	Coaster Name	Height	Length	Speed	# Of Loops	Rate 1 to 5

My Ride Experience:

_____

_____

_____

_____

_____

Roller Coaster Enthusiast Log Book

Amusement Park Name: _____

Location: _____

Date	Coaster Name	Height	Length	Speed	# Of Loops	Rate 1 to 5

My Ride Experience:

_____

_____

_____

_____

Roller Coaster Enthusiast Log Book

Amusement Park Name: _____

Location: _____

Date	Coaster Name	Height	Length	Speed	# Of Loops	Rate 1 to 5

My Ride Experience:

_____

_____

_____

_____

_____

Roller Coaster Enthusiast Log Book

Amusement Park Name: _____

Location: _____

Date	Coaster Name	Height	Length	Speed	# Of Loops	Rate 1 to 5

My Ride Experience:

_____

_____

_____

_____

_____

Roller Coaster Enthusiast Log Book

Amusement Park Name: _____

Location: _____

Date	Coaster Name	Height	Length	Speed	# Of Loops	Rate 1 to 5

My Ride Experience:

_____

_____

_____

_____

_____

Roller Coaster Enthusiast Log Book

Amusement Park Name: _____

Location: _____

Date	Coaster Name	Height	Length	Speed	# Of Loops	Rate 1 to 5

My Ride Experience:

_____

_____

_____

_____

_____

Roller Coaster Enthusiast
Log Book

Amusement Park Name: _____

Location: _____

Date	Coaster Name	Height	Length	Speed	# Of Loops	Rate 1 to 5

My Ride Experience:

_____

_____

_____

_____

_____

Roller Coaster Enthusiast
Log Book

Amusement Park Name: _____

Location: _____

Date	Coaster Name	Height	Length	Speed	# Of Loops	Rate 1 to 5

My Ride Experience:

_____

_____

_____

_____

_____

Roller Coaster Enthusiast Log Book

Amusement Park Name: _____

Location: _____

Date	Coaster Name	Height	Length	Speed	# Of Loops	Rate 1 to 5

My Ride Experience:

_____

_____

_____

_____

_____

Roller Coaster Enthusiast Log Book

Amusement Park Name: _____

Location: _____

Date	Coaster Name	Height	Length	Speed	# Of Loops	Rate 1 to 5

My Ride Experience:

_____

_____

_____

_____

_____

Roller Coaster Enthusiast Log Book

Amusement Park Name: _____

Location: _____

Date	Coaster Name	Height	Length	Speed	# Of Loops	Rate 1 to 5

My Ride Experience:

_____

_____

_____

_____

_____

Roller Coaster Enthusiast Log Book

Amusement Park Name: _____

Location: _____

Date	Coaster Name	Height	Length	Speed	# Of Loops	Rate 1 to 5

My Ride Experience:

_____

_____

_____

_____

_____

Roller Coaster Enthusiast Log Book

Amusement Park Name: _____

Location: _____

Date	Coaster Name	Height	Length	Speed	# Of Loops	Rate 1 to 5

My Ride Experience:

_____

_____

_____

_____

_____

Roller Coaster Enthusiast Log Book

Amusement Park Name: _____

Location: _____

Date	Coaster Name	Height	Length	Speed	# Of Loops	Rate 1 to 5

My Ride Experience:

_____

_____

_____

_____

_____

Roller Coaster Enthusiast Log Book

Amusement Park Name: _____

Location: _____

Date	Coaster Name	Height	Length	Speed	# Of Loops	Rate 1 to 5

My Ride Experience:

_____

_____

_____

_____

_____

Roller Coaster Enthusiast Log Book

Amusement Park Name: _____

Location: _____

Date	Coaster Name	Height	Length	Speed	# Of Loops	Rate 1 to 5

My Ride Experience:

_____

_____

_____

_____

_____

Roller Coaster Enthusiast Log Book

Amusement Park Name: _____

Location: _____

Date	Coaster Name	Height	Length	Speed	# Of Loops	Rate 1 to 5

My Ride Experience:

_____

_____

_____

_____

_____

Roller Coaster Enthusiast Log Book

Amusement Park Name: _____

Location: _____

Date	Coaster Name	Height	Length	Speed	# Of Loops	Rate 1 to 5

My Ride Experience:

_____

_____

_____

_____

_____

Roller Coaster Enthusiast Log Book

Amusement Park Name: _____

Location: _____

Date	Coaster Name	Height	Length	Speed	# Of Loops	Rate 1 to 5

My Ride Experience:

_____

_____

_____

_____

_____

Roller Coaster Enthusiast Log Book

Amusement Park Name: _____

Location: _____

Date	Coaster Name	Height	Length	Speed	# Of Loops	Rate 1 to 5

My Ride Experience:

_____

_____

_____

_____

_____

Roller Coaster Enthusiast Log Book

Amusement Park Name: _____

Location: _____

Date	Coaster Name	Height	Length	Speed	# Of Loops	Rate 1 to 5

My Ride Experience:

_____

_____

_____

_____

_____

Roller Coaster Enthusiast Log Book

Amusement Park Name: _____

Location: _____

Date	Coaster Name	Height	Length	Speed	# Of Loops	Rate 1 to 5

My Ride Experience:

_____

_____

_____

_____

_____

Roller Coaster Enthusiast Log Book

Amusement Park Name: _____

Location: _____

Date	Coaster Name	Height	Length	Speed	# Of Loops	Rate 1 to 5

My Ride Experience:

_____

_____

_____

_____

_____

Roller Coaster Enthusiast Log Book

Amusement Park Name: _____

Location: _____

Date	Coaster Name	Height	Length	Speed	# Of Loops	Rate 1 to 5

My Ride Experience:

_____

_____

_____

_____

_____

Roller Coaster Enthusiast Log Book

Amusement Park Name: _____

Location: _____

Date	Coaster Name	Height	Length	Speed	# Of Loops	Rate 1 to 5

My Ride Experience:

_____

_____

_____

_____

_____

Roller Coaster Enthusiast Log Book

Amusement Park Name: _____

Location: _____

Date	Coaster Name	Height	Length	Speed	# Of Loops	Rate 1 to 5

My Ride Experience:

_____

_____

_____

_____

_____

Roller Coaster Enthusiast Log Book

Amusement Park Name: _____

Location: _____

Date	Coaster Name	Height	Length	Speed	# Of Loops	Rate 1 to 5

My Ride Experience:

_____

_____

_____

_____

_____

Roller Coaster Enthusiast Log Book

Amusement Park Name: _____

Location: _____

Date	Coaster Name	Height	Length	Speed	# Of Loops	Rate 1 to 5

My Ride Experience:

_____

_____

_____

_____

_____

Roller Coaster Enthusiast Log Book

Amusement Park Name: _____

Location: _____

Date	Coaster Name	Height	Length	Speed	# Of Loops	Rate 1 to 5

My Ride Experience:

_____

_____

_____

_____

_____

Roller Coaster Enthusiast Log Book

Amusement Park Name: _____

Location: _____

Date	Coaster Name	Height	Length	Speed	# Of Loops	Rate 1 to 5

My Ride Experience:

_____

_____

_____

_____

Roller Coaster Enthusiast Log Book

Amusement Park Name: _____

Location: _____

Date	Coaster Name	Height	Length	Speed	# Of Loops	Rate 1 to 5

My Ride Experience:

_____

_____

_____

_____

_____

Roller Coaster Enthusiast Log Book

Amusement Park Name: _____

Location: _____

Date	Coaster Name	Height	Length	Speed	# Of Loops	Rate 1 to 5

My Ride Experience:

_____

_____

_____

_____

_____

Roller Coaster Enthusiast Log Book

Amusement Park Name: _____

Location: _____

Date	Coaster Name	Height	Length	Speed	# Of Loops	Rate 1 to 5

My Ride Experience:

_____

_____

_____

_____

_____

Roller Coaster Enthusiast Log Book

Amusement Park Name: _____

Location: _____

Date	Coaster Name	Height	Length	Speed	# Of Loops	Rate 1 to 5

My Ride Experience:

_____

_____

_____

_____

_____

Roller Coaster Enthusiast Log Book

Amusement Park Name: _____

Location: _____

Date	Coaster Name	Height	Length	Speed	# Of Loops	Rate 1 to 5

My Ride Experience:

_____

_____

_____

_____

_____

Roller Coaster Enthusiast Log Book

Amusement Park Name: _____

Location: _____

Date	Coaster Name	Height	Length	Speed	# Of Loops	Rate 1 to 5

My Ride Experience:

_____

_____

_____

_____

_____

Roller Coaster Enthusiast Log Book

Amusement Park Name: _____

Location: _____

Date	Coaster Name	Height	Length	Speed	# Of Loops	Rate 1 to 5

My Ride Experience:

_____

_____

_____

_____

_____

Roller Coaster Enthusiast Log Book

Amusement Park Name: _____

Location: _____

Date	Coaster Name	Height	Length	Speed	# Of Loops	Rate 1 to 5

My Ride Experience:

_____

_____

_____

_____

_____

Roller Coaster Enthusiast Log Book

Amusement Park Name: _____

Location: _____

Date	Coaster Name	Height	Length	Speed	# Of Loops	Rate 1 to 5

My Ride Experience:

_____

_____

_____

_____

_____

Roller Coaster Enthusiast Log Book

Amusement Park Name: _____

Location: _____

Date	Coaster Name	Height	Length	Speed	# Of Loops	Rate 1 to 5

My Ride Experience:

_____

_____

_____

_____

_____

Roller Coaster Enthusiast Log Book

Amusement Park Name: _____

Location: _____

Date	Coaster Name	Height	Length	Speed	# Of Loops	Rate 1 to 5

My Ride Experience:

_____

_____

_____

_____

Roller Coaster Enthusiast Log Book

Amusement Park Name: _____

Location: _____

Date	Coaster Name	Height	Length	Speed	# Of Loops	Rate 1 to 5

My Ride Experience:

_____

_____

_____

_____

_____

Roller Coaster Enthusiast Log Book

Amusement Park Name: _____

Location: _____

Date	Coaster Name	Height	Length	Speed	# Of Loops	Rate 1 to 5

My Ride Experience:

_____

_____

_____

_____

_____

Roller Coaster Enthusiast Log Book

Amusement Park Name: _____

Location: _____

Date	Coaster Name	Height	Length	Speed	# Of Loops	Rate 1 to 5

My Ride Experience:

_____

_____

_____

_____

_____

Roller Coaster Enthusiast Log Book

Amusement Park Name: _____

Location: _____

Date	Coaster Name	Height	Length	Speed	# Of Loops	Rate 1 to 5

My Ride Experience:

_____

_____

_____

_____

_____

Roller Coaster Enthusiast Log Book

Amusement Park Name: _____

Location: _____

Date	Coaster Name	Height	Length	Speed	# Of Loops	Rate 1 to 5

My Ride Experience:

_____

_____

_____

_____

_____

Roller Coaster Enthusiast Log Book

Amusement Park Name: _____

Location: _____

Date	Coaster Name	Height	Length	Speed	# Of Loops	Rate 1 to 5

My Ride Experience:

_____

_____

_____

_____

_____

Roller Coaster Enthusiast Log Book

Amusement Park Name: _____

Location: _____

Date	Coaster Name	Height	Length	Speed	# Of Loops	Rate 1 to 5

My Ride Experience:

_____

_____

_____

_____

_____

Roller Coaster Enthusiast Log Book

Amusement Park Name: _____

Location: _____

Date	Coaster Name	Height	Length	Speed	# Of Loops	Rate 1 to 5

My Ride Experience:

_____

_____

_____

_____

_____

Roller Coaster Enthusiast Log Book

Amusement Park Name: _____

Location: _____

Date	Coaster Name	Height	Length	Speed	# Of Loops	Rate 1 to 5

My Ride Experience:

_____

_____

_____

_____

_____

Roller Coaster Enthusiast Log Book

Amusement Park Name: _____

Location: _____

Date	Coaster Name	Height	Length	Speed	# Of Loops	Rate 1 to 5

My Ride Experience:

_____

_____

_____

_____

_____

Roller Coaster Enthusiast Log Book

Amusement Park Name: _____

Location: _____

Date	Coaster Name	Height	Length	Speed	# Of Loops	Rate 1 to 5

My Ride Experience:

_____

_____

_____

_____

_____

Roller Coaster Enthusiast Log Book

Amusement Park Name: _____

Location: _____

Date	Coaster Name	Height	Length	Speed	# Of Loops	Rate 1 to 5

My Ride Experience:

_____

_____

_____

_____

_____

Roller Coaster Enthusiast Log Book

Amusement Park Name: _____

Location: _____

Date	Coaster Name	Height	Length	Speed	# Of Loops	Rate 1 to 5

My Ride Experience:

_____

_____

_____

_____

_____

Roller Coaster Enthusiast Log Book

Amusement Park Name: _____

Location: _____

Date	Coaster Name	Height	Length	Speed	# Of Loops	Rate 1 to 5

My Ride Experience:

_____

_____

_____

_____

_____

Roller Coaster Enthusiast Log Book

Amusement Park Name: _____

Location: _____

Date	Coaster Name	Height	Length	Speed	# Of Loops	Rate 1 to 5

My Ride Experience:

_____

_____

_____

_____

_____

Roller Coaster Enthusiast Log Book

Amusement Park Name: _____

Location: _____

Date	Coaster Name	Height	Length	Speed	# Of Loops	Rate 1 to 5

My Ride Experience:

_____

_____

_____

_____

_____

Roller Coaster Enthusiast Log Book

Amusement Park Name: _____

Location: _____

Date	Coaster Name	Height	Length	Speed	# Of Loops	Rate 1 to 5

My Ride Experience:

_____

_____

_____

_____

_____

Roller Coaster Enthusiast
Log Book

Amusement Park Name: _____

Location: _____

Date	Coaster Name	Height	Length	Speed	# Of Loops	Rate 1 to 5

My Ride Experience:

_____

_____

_____

_____

_____

Roller Coaster Enthusiast Log Book

Amusement Park Name: _____

Location: _____

Date	Coaster Name	Height	Length	Speed	# Of Loops	Rate 1 to 5

My Ride Experience:

_____

_____

_____

_____

_____

Roller Coaster Enthusiast Log Book

Amusement Park Name: _____

Location: _____

Date	Coaster Name	Height	Length	Speed	# Of Loops	Rate 1 to 5

My Ride Experience:

_____

_____

_____

_____

_____

Roller Coaster Enthusiast Log Book

Amusement Park Name: _____

Location: _____

Date	Coaster Name	Height	Length	Speed	# Of Loops	Rate 1 to 5

My Ride Experience:

_____

_____

_____

_____

_____

Roller Coaster Enthusiast Log Book

Amusement Park Name: _____

Location: _____

Date	Coaster Name	Height	Length	Speed	# Of Loops	Rate 1 to 5

My Ride Experience:

_____

_____

_____

_____

_____

Roller Coaster Enthusiast Log Book

Amusement Park Name: _____

Location: _____

Date	Coaster Name	Height	Length	Speed	# Of Loops	Rate 1 to 5

My Ride Experience:

_____

_____

_____

_____

_____

Roller Coaster Enthusiast Log Book

Amusement Park Name: _____

Location: _____

Date	Coaster Name	Height	Length	Speed	# Of Loops	Rate 1 to 5

My Ride Experience:

_____

_____

_____

_____

_____

Roller Coaster Enthusiast Log Book

Amusement Park Name: _____

Location: _____

Date	Coaster Name	Height	Length	Speed	# Of Loops	Rate 1 to 5

My Ride Experience:

_____

_____

_____

_____

_____

Roller Coaster Enthusiast Log Book

Amusement Park Name: _____

Location: _____

Date	Coaster Name	Height	Length	Speed	# Of Loops	Rate 1 to 5

My Ride Experience:

_____

_____

_____

_____

_____

Roller Coaster Enthusiast Log Book

Amusement Park Name: _____

Location: _____

Date	Coaster Name	Height	Length	Speed	# Of Loops	Rate 1 to 5

My Ride Experience:

_____

_____

_____

_____

Roller Coaster Enthusiast Log Book

Amusement Park Name: _____

Location: _____

Date	Coaster Name	Height	Length	Speed	# Of Loops	Rate 1 to 5

My Ride Experience:

_____

_____

_____

_____

_____

Roller Coaster Enthusiast Log Book

Amusement Park Name: _____

Location: _____

Date	Coaster Name	Height	Length	Speed	# Of Loops	Rate 1 to 5

My Ride Experience:

_____

_____

_____

_____

_____

Roller Coaster Enthusiast Log Book

Amusement Park Name: _____

Location: _____

Date	Coaster Name	Height	Length	Speed	# Of Loops	Rate 1 to 5

My Ride Experience:

_____

_____

_____

_____

_____

Roller Coaster Enthusiast Log Book

Amusement Park Name: _____

Location: _____

Date	Coaster Name	Height	Length	Speed	# Of Loops	Rate 1 to 5

My Ride Experience:

_____

_____

_____

_____

_____

Roller Coaster Enthusiast Log Book

Amusement Park Name: _____

Location: _____

Date	Coaster Name	Height	Length	Speed	# Of Loops	Rate 1 to 5

My Ride Experience:

_____

_____

_____

_____

_____

Roller Coaster Enthusiast Log Book

Amusement Park Name: _____

Location: _____

Date	Coaster Name	Height	Length	Speed	# Of Loops	Rate 1 to 5

My Ride Experience:

_____

_____

_____

_____

_____

Roller Coaster Enthusiast Log Book

Amusement Park Name: _____

Location: _____

Date	Coaster Name	Height	Length	Speed	# Of Loops	Rate 1 to 5

My Ride Experience:

_____

_____

_____

_____

_____

Roller Coaster Enthusiast
Log Book

Amusement Park Name: _____

Location: _____

Date	Coaster Name	Height	Length	Speed	# Of Loops	Rate 1 to 5

My Ride Experience:

_____

_____

_____

_____

_____

Roller Coaster Enthusiast Log Book

Amusement Park Name: _____

Location: _____

Date	Coaster Name	Height	Length	Speed	# Of Loops	Rate 1 to 5

My Ride Experience:

_____

_____

_____

_____

_____

Roller Coaster Enthusiast Log Book

Amusement Park Name: _____

Location: _____

Date	Coaster Name	Height	Length	Speed	# Of Loops	Rate 1 to 5

My Ride Experience:

_____

_____

_____

_____

_____

Roller Coaster Enthusiast Log Book

Amusement Park Name: _____

Location: _____

Date	Coaster Name	Height	Length	Speed	# Of Loops	Rate 1 to 5

My Ride Experience:

_____

_____

_____

_____

_____

Roller Coaster Enthusiast Log Book

Amusement Park Name: _____

Location: _____

Date	Coaster Name	Height	Length	Speed	# Of Loops	Rate 1 to 5

My Ride Experience:

_____

_____

_____

_____

_____

Roller Coaster Enthusiast Log Book

Amusement Park Name: _____

Location: _____

Date	Coaster Name	Height	Length	Speed	# Of Loops	Rate 1 to 5

My Ride Experience:

_____

_____

_____

_____

_____

Roller Coaster Enthusiast Log Book

Amusement Park Name: _____

Location: _____

Date	Coaster Name	Height	Length	Speed	# Of Loops	Rate 1 to 5

My Ride Experience:

_____

_____

_____

_____

_____

Roller Coaster Enthusiast Log Book

Amusement Park Name: _____

Location: _____

Date	Coaster Name	Height	Length	Speed	# Of Loops	Rate 1 to 5

My Ride Experience:

_____

_____

_____

_____

_____

Roller Coaster Enthusiast Log Book

Amusement Park Name: _____

Location: _____

Date	Coaster Name	Height	Length	Speed	# Of Loops	Rate 1 to 5

My Ride Experience:

_____

_____

_____

_____

_____

Roller Coaster Enthusiast Log Book

Amusement Park Name: _____

Location: _____

Date	Coaster Name	Height	Length	Speed	# Of Loops	Rate 1 to 5

My Ride Experience:

_____

_____

_____

_____

_____

Roller Coaster Enthusiast Log Book

Amusement Park Name: _____

Location: _____

Date	Coaster Name	Height	Length	Speed	# Of Loops	Rate 1 to 5

My Ride Experience:

_____

_____

_____

_____

_____

Roller Coaster Enthusiast Log Book

Amusement Park Name: _____

Location: _____

Date	Coaster Name	Height	Length	Speed	# Of Loops	Rate 1 to 5

My Ride Experience:

_____

_____

_____

_____

_____

Roller Coaster Enthusiast Log Book

Amusement Park Name: _____

Location: _____

Date	Coaster Name	Height	Length	Speed	# Of Loops	Rate 1 to 5

My Ride Experience:

_____

_____

_____

_____

_____

Roller Coaster Enthusiast
Log Book

Amusement Park Name: _____

Location: _____

Date	Coaster Name	Height	Length	Speed	# Of Loops	Rate 1 to 5

My Ride Experience:

_____

_____

_____

_____

_____

Roller Coaster Enthusiast Log Book

Amusement Park Name: _____

Location: _____

Date	Coaster Name	Height	Length	Speed	# Of Loops	Rate 1 to 5

My Ride Experience:

_____

_____

_____

_____

_____

Roller Coaster Enthusiast Log Book

Amusement Park Name: _____

Location: _____

Date	Coaster Name	Height	Length	Speed	# Of Loops	Rate 1 to 5

My Ride Experience:

_____

_____

_____

_____

_____

Roller Coaster Enthusiast Log Book

Amusement Park Name: _____

Location: _____

Date	Coaster Name	Height	Length	Speed	# Of Loops	Rate 1 to 5

My Ride Experience:

_____

_____

_____

_____

_____

Made in the USA
Columbia, SC
17 December 2022

74377874R00067